THE ILLUSION OF CONTROL

WHY WE CHASE POWER, AND WHAT IT COSTS US

YUDHISHTHIR SHARMA

THE ILLUSION OF CONTROL

Acknowledgement

This book was not written alone—though many pages were typed in solitude, it was shaped by countless conversations, encouragements, and truths shared by others.

To the friends, mentors, and colleagues who challenged my thinking and shared their own stories of control, burnout, and breakthrough— thank you for your honesty. Your lived experiences gave this book its heartbeat.

To my family: your support, patience, and grounding love gave me the freedom to explore these themes deeply and vulnerably. You reminded me that letting go doesn't mean giving up—it means making room for something truer.

To the readers, thinkers, and seekers who've wrestled with the same questions—this book is for you. I hope it meets you where you are, and helps you breathe a little easier in the uncertainty.

And finally, to those I've tried to control, knowingly or not: thank you for your grace. You taught me what this book could never say directly— that real connection begins where control ends.

Title: The Illusion of Control: Why We Chase Power, and What It Costs Us

Preface: The Quiet Obsession

Have you ever wondered why we need to be in control? Not just of others, but of situations, plans, outcomes—even conversations? We try to forecast markets, micromanage teams, overthink relationships, and map out the next five years like we're gods with a spreadsheet. But the truth? Control is often just an illusion we cling to in a chaotic world.

This book was born from late-night corporate calls that ran over, from watching good people burn out while trying to "manage" things beyond their power, and from moments of deep personal reflection—where I realized how often I've chased control at the cost of joy, connection, or clarity. This is not a self-help book telling you to "let go and let God." Nor is it a manual on how to be more powerful. It's an honest, inside-out journey into why we chase control, how it shows up in our work and lives, and what it quietly costs us—our peace, our relationships, and sometimes, our integrity. So, let's get into it. No jargon. Just real stories, real people, and a bit of hard truth.

Chapter 1: Born to Control – The Human Urge

Let's start at the beginning—why do we crave control in the first place?

Psychologists call it the "control heuristic." It's our brain's way of feeling safe. When we think we're in control, anxiety drops. It's evolutionary. In the wild, early humans who anticipated threats and acted to control their environment—by building shelter, storing food, or forming alliances—were the ones who survived.

Fast-forward to the 21st century. Our predators aren't tigers anymore. They're deadlines, difficult bosses, volatile markets, and unpredictable relationships. But the instinct to control? Still hardwired.

The Corporate Example: The Manager Who Couldn't Let Go

Let me tell you about Rahul, a mid-level manager in a top FMCG firm. Brilliant guy. Ivy League degree. Promoted twice in five years. But behind the scenes? He was drowning.

Rahul couldn't delegate. He double-checked everything his team submitted. He worked late hours not because he had to, but because he didn't *trust* that things would go right without his eyes on them.

Eventually, his team disengaged. They stopped putting in their best because they knew he'd rewrite their work anyway. The irony? In trying to stay in control, Rahul lost the one thing control was supposed to bring: performance.

It's not uncommon. Many corporate leaders fall into this trap. They equate control with competence, when in reality, it often becomes a bottleneck.

Control Feels Safer Than Chaos

Even outside the office, think of how often we make plans, not for fun, but to reduce uncertainty.

Ever mapped out a vacation to the hour, only to get annoyed when something didn't go according to schedule? That's your brain protesting against the discomfort of unpredictability. But unpredictability is life. The same pattern plays out in personal relationships. People try to change their partners, plan every step of a wedding, or "control" their kids' futures. It rarely ends well.

The Paradox: Here's the paradox no one tells us:
the more we chase control, the more anxious we
become. Because deep down, we know—things will
still go wrong. People will still surprise us. Plans will
still shift. Control gives us a momentary sense of
power, not real peace.

Chapter 2: Control in the Corporate Cage

Walk into any modern office, and the illusion of control is on full display. There are calendars color-coded down to the minute, spreadsheets that model outcomes to the third decimal place, and performance reviews designed to measure the unmeasurable: effort, motivation, potential.

Control is not just encouraged in corporate life—it's institutionalized. Job titles, reporting lines, KPIs, and org charts are all symbolic scaffolding erected to impose order on the unpredictability of human behavior. But underneath the surface, control often functions less as a tool for clarity and more as a shield against uncertainty—and even against each other.

The Myth of Managerial Omniscience

Management, especially middle management, is often cast in the role of the all-seeing eye: responsible for anticipating risks, allocating resources, and ensuring everyone is "on track." But the modern workplace moves too fast and is too complex for any one person—or even one team—to fully control.

This breeds a kind of existential tension. Leaders feel pressure to appear in command, even when they're making decisions based on incomplete information. Employees sense this, and many respond by trying to control what little they can—emails, Slack messages, calendar invites—leading to overcommunication, underperformance, and a creeping sense of distrust.

Micromanagement is often a symptom of fear. The more we sense chaos at the macro level—economic instability, layoffs, global competition—the more tightly we grip the levers of day-to-day activity, often to the detriment of creativity and morale.

Power, Perception, and Pretending

Ironically, the higher up someone is in the hierarchy, the more control they are *perceived* to have—and the less they often feel. CEOs don't control markets. Executives don't control consumer behavior. What they control, mostly, are narratives.

The corporate world runs not just on strategy, but on illusion. The illusion that someone is in charge. That someone knows the plan. That someone has the answer. Maintaining this illusion is emotionally expensive, especially for leaders who feel they must wear the mask of certainty even when filled with doubt.

And so, the system self-replicates: leaders pretend to know, employees pretend to trust, and everyone stays locked in a performance of stability that masks the underlying chaos.

The Cost: Burnout and Bureaucracy

The psychological toll of this dynamic is enormous. Employees subjected to rigid oversight often experience decision fatigue, resentment, or quiet disengagement. Leaders under pressure to control outcomes they cannot predict suffer from burnout, anxiety, and isolation. When the measure of success is flawless execution of a rigid plan, failure becomes personal—and inevitable.

Bureaucracy, meant to streamline and standardize, often becomes a bottleneck. The pursuit of control spawns process after process, meeting after meeting, and document after document—all in the name of alignment. But alignment without trust becomes compliance without creativity.

The Alternative: Influence Over Control

True leadership doesn't come from control—it comes from influence. The most effective leaders today recognize the limits of micromanagement and instead focus on creating environments of psychological safety, autonomy, and shared purpose. They know they can't control outcomes—but they can shape conditions.

The future of work belongs not to those who grip harder, but to those who learn to let go. Who replace domination with direction. Who stop pretending to be in control, and start learning how to respond wisely to complexity.

Control may win compliance, but only influence earns commitment.

Chapter 3: The Cost of Control – Burnout, Betrayal & Blind Spots

Control promises security, but often delivers exhaustion. It's sold as a path to power, but frequently becomes a road to disconnection. The human toll of obsessive control is rarely accounted for—until it shows up in the breakdowns we can no longer ignore.

Whether in the workplace, in relationships, or in our own minds, the cost of control reveals itself in three key symptoms: **burnout**, **betrayal**, and **blind spots**. Each is a signal—a warning light that we are pushing past the limits of what control can actually deliver.

Burnout: When Control Becomes a Burden

Burnout is not just overwork—it's the psychic weight of responsibility without relief. People who seek control often take on more than they should. They don't delegate. They don't trust. They can't rest. The mindset is simple and toxic: "If I don't do it, it won't get done right."

Over time, this creates a grinding internal pressure. Days feel tight, nights become restless. Even small tasks feel monumental. Ironically, the more burned out we become, the more we double down on control—trying to fix the problem by working harder, tightening the screws, and eliminating uncertainty.

Control, in this case, becomes a kind of addiction: it temporarily soothes the anxiety it helped create. But like all addictions, it eventually stops working.

Betrayal: When Control Erodes Trust

To control others is to assume they cannot be trusted. And over time, that assumption becomes reality. People respond to control with resistance or resentment. The more you monitor, manage, and manipulate, the less others feel safe or seen.

This is especially true in close relationships. A partner who insists on controlling decisions may believe they are "helping" or "protecting," but to the other person, it feels like suffocation. Parents who micromanage their children's lives often create dependence instead of resilience. Friends who try to dictate the flow of conversations or plans create distance instead of connection.

Betrayal happens subtly, and often unintentionally. We don't mean to push people away. But when we make them feel small, incompetent, or invisible, they eventually leave—not out of malice, but out of self-preservation.

And when they do, we feel betrayed. But often, the betrayal began with our inability to relinquish control.

Blind Spots: When Control Distorts Reality

Perhaps the most dangerous cost of control is what we stop seeing. Control narrows focus. It creates tunnel vision. We become so preoccupied with ensuring outcomes that we ignore new information, dismiss alternative perspectives, and overlook emerging threats or opportunities.

Blind spots form when we mistake control for clarity. We stop asking questions. We filter out dissent. We prefer the comfort of certainty over the discomfort of truth. Leaders who cling to control often surround themselves with yes-men. Individuals who demand control in personal life avoid feedback, fearing the collapse of their fragile self-image.

History is littered with stories of collapses—companies, governments, relationships—brought down not by enemies, but by unseen flaws left unacknowledged for too long. And control, for all its promises, can be the very thing that blocks the vision we need to adapt, grow, and survive.

What the Costs Reveal

Burnout, betrayal, and blind spots are not failures of strategy—they are signals of misalignment. They tell us that our quest for control has exceeded our capacity for flexibility, connection, and humility. They remind us that power, when pursued without self-awareness, becomes a trap.

To see the true cost of control is not to condemn it entirely—but to approach it with discernment. Control is not inherently evil. It can be a useful tool. But when it becomes the default mode of living, leading, and relating, it extracts more than it gives.

In the next chapter, we'll zoom in on how control plays out in our closest relationships—where its effects are often the most invisible, and the most profound.

Chapter 4: Power Games in Personal Relationships

We often think of control as a workplace issue, or a political dynamic—but some of the deepest, most damaging forms of control happen behind closed doors, in the relationships we claim are built on love.

Romantic partners, parents, friends, and even adult children can fall into patterns of domination masked as devotion. Unlike corporate control, which is often formalized and visible, interpersonal control hides in the everyday. It's a suggestion laced with guilt, a boundary disguised as a favor, a "concern" that feels like surveillance.

These power games rarely start with malice. They usually grow from fear—fear of abandonment, of rejection, of losing influence. But when control becomes a substitute for communication, relationships slowly corrode from the inside out.

Love vs. Control

One of the most dangerous myths we inherit is that love and control go hand in hand. "I just want what's best for you," becomes code for "I want you to do what I think is best." We confuse care with correction, support with surveillance, protection with possession.

But real love does not require control. Real love allows for autonomy. It respects difference. It accepts uncertainty. Control, by contrast, demands compliance. It treats the other person as a project, a problem, or a possession. It tries to engineer outcomes instead of embracing experience.

This is especially visible in relationships where one person takes on a caretaker role—whether due to personality, tradition, or perceived maturity. The intention may be noble. But the result is often subtle coercion: an ongoing pressure for the other to change, improve, or conform in order to maintain harmony.

Emotional Manipulation: The Invisible Reins

Control in personal relationships often wears the mask of emotional intelligence. It's not just about shouting orders or issuing ultimatums. It's the silent treatment used as punishment. The guilt trip disguised as concern. The insistence on "just being honest" when the goal is to hurt, not heal.

Emotional manipulation thrives in ambiguity. It creates a fog in which the controlled person begins to doubt their own perceptions. "Maybe I am overreacting." "Maybe I do need to change." Over time, they internalize the controller's voice as their own. What began as subtle influence becomes silent dominance.

The controller, meanwhile, may be unaware of their own tactics. They tell themselves they're simply more "mature," more "rational," or more "invested." They may even feel victimized when their partner, friend, or child pulls away. But their need to manage emotional outcomes has created an environment where trust cannot breathe.

Control as a Substitute for Intimacy

Here's the irony: the more we control, the less connected we feel. Control creates performance, not intimacy. People act the part they think is expected, rather than show up as they are. Conversations become negotiations. Vulnerability becomes risky. Honesty gets filtered through fear.

Control kills the thing it claims to protect.

True intimacy requires a kind of surrender—of being seen without guarantees, of loving without leashes. It demands that we stop managing impressions and start risking truth.

But for many, that level of exposure feels unbearable. And so control becomes the fallback—an armor against emotional nakedness.

How to Recognize the Patterns

Control in personal relationships often follows a pattern:

- **Unspoken expectations:** You expect someone to act a certain way but never communicate it directly.

- **Withholding behavior:** You give or withhold affection, attention, or approval to influence outcomes.

- **Boundary violation:** You override someone's preferences in the name of "helping" or "knowing better."

- **Emotional reactivity:** You respond to disagreement with disproportionate anger, guilt, or silence.

These patterns are not about love—they are about fear. And once we see them, we can begin to change them.

From Control to Connection

The antidote to control is not chaos. It's conscious connection. It's learning to sit with uncertainty, to honor the agency of others, and to value truth over comfort.

This requires work—often painful, always humbling. It means taking responsibility for our own needs, rather than outsourcing them to others through control. It means practicing boundaries without manipulation. And it means recognizing that love, at its best, is not a transaction. It's a trust fall.

Relationships built on trust may not always feel predictable. But they are real. They breathe. They grow.

In the next chapter, we'll explore how the digital world magnifies our craving for control—and how the promise of freedom online often turns into a new kind of prison.

Chapter 5: The Illusion of Freedom in the Digital Age

We were promised liberation. The internet would democratize information. Social media would give everyone a voice. Smart devices would free us from the mundane, automate the complex, and deliver convenience at the tap of a screen.

And in many ways, they did.

But somewhere along the way, the tools of freedom became instruments of surveillance, self-obsession, and subtle control. We can now edit our lives in real time—every photo filtered, every opinion curated, every moment optimized. We are more connected than ever, yet more fragmented, anxious, and beholden to algorithms we don't understand.

In the digital age, we appear to have more control than any generation before us. But it is a control built on performance, not presence. On personalization, not autonomy. On data, not understanding.

And perhaps most importantly: it is a control that increasingly controls us.

The Illusion of Choice

At first glance, the digital world is a paradise of options. Thousands of products, shows, books, courses—anything, anytime. But choice does not equal freedom. In fact, too many choices can paralyze us, distract us, or push us toward the path of least resistance: what's popular, trending, or recommended.

Algorithms filter what we see based on past behavior. Search engines tailor results based on geography, history, and preference. Social platforms nudge us toward outrage, engagement, and addictive scrolling. The more we use these tools, the more they learn about us—until our future is shaped by our past, and novelty becomes an illusion.

What we call *customization* is often *conditioning*. And what we believe to be free will may be little more than digital momentum.

The Quantified Self

We now track everything—our steps, sleep, heart rate, productivity, even our mood. We measure ourselves into oblivion, hoping that more data will give us more control over our bodies, minds, and time.

But tracking can easily become tyranny.

The smartwatch doesn't just tell us how we slept—it tells us how to feel about how we slept. The calendar doesn't just organize our day—it judges our value by how full it is. Even rest becomes something to optimize, as though stillness needs a score.

What begins as self-awareness can mutate into self-surveillance. We become our own warden, obsessively checking for signs of progress, performance, and proof that we are enough.

And beneath it all lies the same ancient fear: that without control, we are vulnerable, lost, or unworthy.

Social Media: The Theater of Control

On social platforms, we control how we appear—but at a cost. We curate what to post, filter how we look, manage how we sound. We edit ourselves to fit the algorithm and the audience.

But the more we perfect our image, the more detached we become from who we really are. Vulnerability becomes a performance. Authenticity becomes a brand. Even rebellion is commodified.

What looks like self-expression is often self-presentation. What feels like freedom is often a new kind of captivity—one where the prison is invisible and the warden is inside our head.

And the irony? We're all doing it. Pretending not to care while deeply invested in likes, views, and reach. Crafting authenticity for approval. Seeking connection through control.

Who's in Control?

The deeper question isn't just whether we control our devices—it's whether they control *us*. Not in some dystopian, sci-fi way, but in subtle shifts of attention, behavior, and identity.

When we wake up and check our phones before we breathe consciously, who's in control?

When a ping overrides a conversation, a scroll replaces solitude, or a post dictates our mood—who's in control?

When we rely on GPS even when we know the way, when we default to screens to avoid silence, when we outsource memory to machines—what part of our humanity are we trading for convenience?

These aren't questions of blame, but of awareness. The problem isn't technology itself—it's our unconscious relationship to it. It's how we've come to equate visibility with value, metrics with meaning, and control with connection.

Reclaiming Freedom

Real freedom begins not with more control, but with better discernment. It's the ability to *choose* how we relate to our tools, rather than letting them shape us invisibly. It means recognizing when convenience crosses into dependency, when customization slides into coercion, and when performance eclipses presence.

It means making space for boredom, silence, and the slow, analog messiness of real life.

It means remembering that to be human is not to be optimized—it's to be alive, uncertain, evolving.

Control in the digital age is seductive because it feels like freedom. But the deeper freedom lies in learning to let go—of needing to be always seen, always measuring, always right.

In the next chapter, we'll explore a critical distinction that can help us navigate both power and peace: the difference between **control** and **influence**—and why knowing that difference changes everything.

Chapter 6: Control vs. Influence – Knowing the Difference

We often confuse control with influence. They can look similar from the outside—both involve trying to shape outcomes, guide behavior, or lead others toward a vision. But their core mechanisms are fundamentally different.

Control demands obedience. Influence invites alignment.

Control is fear-driven—it seeks to prevent chaos. Influence is trust-driven—it seeks to create meaning.

Understanding the difference isn't just intellectual— it's transformative. When we stop trying to control everything, we create space for influence to do its deeper work. We become more effective, more respected, and more human.

Control Grips. Influence Opens.

Control is about force—exerting pressure, imposing rules, setting rigid expectations. It relies on authority, leverage, or fear of consequences. It gets short-term compliance but breeds long-term resistance.

Influence, by contrast, operates through credibility, consistency, and clarity. It's not about forcing behavior but about shaping belief. It doesn't impose; it inspires. Where control pushes, influence pulls.

Think of a boss who micromanages every move versus one who leads by example, communicates vision, and listens with intent. The former gets results—sometimes—but often at the cost of morale and innovation. The latter builds loyalty, creativity, and resilience.

Influence is slower, yes. But it's deeper, and it lasts.

The Roots of Each

Control often emerges from insecurity—the fear of failure, loss, or unpredictability. When we don't trust the process (or people), we default to control as a defense mechanism.

Influence grows from confidence—not the loud, performative kind, but the quiet, inner certainty that knows its values and doesn't panic in uncertainty. People who operate from influence are less reactive. They're curious, not combative. They know that outcomes can't be guaranteed, but direction can be shaped.

You can't influence people you don't respect. And you can't respect people you're trying to control.

Parenting, Leadership, and Personal Power

Whether you're raising a child, leading a team, or managing a crisis, the temptation to control is universal. But over time, influence proves far more powerful.

- **Parents** who influence teach through modeling, conversation, and boundaries rooted in love. Parents who control demand conformity, often at the expense of trust and long-term autonomy.

- **Leaders** who influence build cultures of ownership. Leaders who control create systems of surveillance.

- **Partners** who influence offer presence, perspective, and mutual growth. Partners who control create emotional debt, power games, and learned helplessness.

The moment you stop needing to dominate a person or situation is the moment you gain the capacity to shape it meaningfully.

The Hidden Power of Non-Attachment

A secret weapon of influence is **non-attachment**. Not indifference—but a willingness to act without clinging to the outcome. This is where real leadership lives: in the paradox of commitment without control.

When you trust your intention, you don't need to force every result. You show up, speak clearly, act with integrity—and let go.

This doesn't mean passivity. It means power without panic.

Ironically, the less we try to control people, the more likely they are to trust, listen, and follow. Influence respects autonomy. And autonomy builds loyalty.

From Domination to Direction

The shift from control to influence is subtle but profound:

- From demanding outcomes → to co-creating possibilities

- From fearing mistakes → to welcoming learning

- From issuing commands → to asking questions

- From managing others → to managing your presence

It requires self-awareness, emotional regulation, and humility. But it also brings a kind of freedom: the freedom to lead without pretending to be invincible, to guide without manipulation, to care without possession.

Influence is the quiet force behind every lasting change. It's how cultures evolve, how movements rise, and how trust is built one conversation at a time.

In the next chapter, we'll explore what happens when even well-meaning control goes wrong—when the very strategies we use to gain security or success end up producing the opposite.

Chapter 7: When Control Backfires – Case Studies

Control promises safety, success, and stability. But when pushed too far, it often breeds the very chaos it tries to avoid. In this chapter, we explore what happens when control backfires—not in theory, but in real life. Through case studies from business, politics, personal life, and culture, we'll see how the overuse of control leads to breakdowns in trust, performance, and sustainability.

Each case tells the same deeper story: control creates diminishing returns—and eventually, destruction.

Case Study 1: The Micromanaging CEO

Background:
A high-performing tech startup, led by a brilliant but anxious founder, begins to scale rapidly. As new teams are added, the founder becomes increasingly controlling—requiring daily reports, personally approving small decisions, and second-guessing department leads.

What Happened:

Initially, this control looked like dedication. Investors praised the founder's "hands-on leadership." But within a year, executive turnover spiked, employee engagement dropped, and innovation stalled. People stopped offering new ideas because they assumed the founder would override them.

When Control Backfired:

By trying to ensure perfection, the CEO became a bottleneck. What had worked at 10 people collapsed at 100. The very behaviors that drove early success created later dysfunction. It wasn't until the founder was forced to step back—for health reasons—that the company regained its creative momentum.

Lesson:

Control does not scale. Influence does.

Case Study 2: The Helicopter Parent

Background:

A well-meaning parent wants to protect her teenage daughter from failure. She manages her schedule, proofreads her homework, chooses her extracurriculars, and intervenes in conflicts with teachers and friends.

What Happened:

On paper, the daughter excels. Straight A's, no major problems. But by college, she collapses under the pressure of independence. She struggles to make decisions, handle failure, or advocate for herself. She calls home multiple times a day, seeking constant reassurance.

When Control Backfired:

The parent controlled for success but unintentionally blocked the development of resilience. In protecting her daughter from discomfort, she deprived her of essential growth.

Lesson:

Control may prevent short-term pain—but it can stunt long-term development.

Case Study 3: The Controlling Romantic Partner

Background:

A man in a long-term relationship begins subtly controlling his partner's decisions—offering "advice" about her friends, discouraging time apart, making financial decisions unilaterally. He believes he's being protective and responsible.

What Happened:

His partner starts to withdraw emotionally. Arguments increase. She feels suffocated but can't fully articulate why. Eventually, she ends the relationship, citing a loss of autonomy and trust.

When Control Backfired:

The partner's attempt to build closeness through control destroyed the very intimacy he craved. His "protection" was perceived as possession.

Lesson:

Love cannot flourish where freedom is denied.

Case Study 4: The Algorithm Gone Rogue

Background:

A major social media platform develops an algorithm to increase engagement. It prioritizes content that triggers strong emotional reactions—anger, outrage, tribalism—because those keep people scrolling.

What Happened:

Engagement soars, ad revenue climbs. But within a few years, the platform is blamed for polarizing public discourse, spreading misinformation, and inciting real-world violence. Governments intervene. Public trust collapses.

When Control Backfired:

An attempt to control user behavior through engineered incentives led to unintended consequences. The algorithm didn't understand ethics—it understood attention.

Lesson:

Control through design must be tempered by responsibility. Influence without conscience becomes manipulation.

Case Study 5: The Perfectionist Self

Background:
A high-achieving woman applies strict control to herself—perfect diet, perfect schedule, perfect performance. She builds a "flawless" life: accolades, promotions, admiration.

What Happened:
Privately, she is exhausted, lonely, and increasingly numb. She avoids emotional vulnerability, sees rest as weakness, and fears that if she lets go even slightly, everything will fall apart.

When Control Backfired:
Her self-control, once a source of strength, becomes a prison. The pursuit of perfection isolates her from joy, intimacy, and peace.

Lesson:
Self-control without self-compassion is a slow form of self-destruction.

Patterns Behind the Failures

Though these stories differ in context, the pattern is consistent:

- Control often begins with good intentions.

- It works—briefly.

- Then it breeds dependency, resistance, or dysfunction.

- The more it's enforced, the more brittle things become.

- Eventually, something breaks.

When control backfires, it reveals the truth we've been avoiding: outcomes are not always ours to command. People are not problems to solve. Systems are not static. And life cannot be fully tamed.

In the next chapter, we'll explore the radical idea that freedom might lie not in more control—but in **letting go**.

Chapter 8: Letting Go – The Power of Surrender

Surrender is not a word that sits easily in modern life. It sounds like failure. Weakness. Giving up. But real surrender isn't about apathy or inaction. It's about releasing the illusion that we can control everything—and finding peace, power, and clarity in what remains.

Letting go is not passive. It is an active, courageous choice. It's choosing trust over tension. Presence over performance. Influence over interference. And most importantly: reality over illusion.

After chapters of exploring how control plays out—at work, in relationships, in society, and within ourselves—this chapter marks the turning point: not just in thought, but in practice.

The Myth of the Grip

We believe that holding tighter makes us safer. That if we just plan better, discipline harder, anticipate more, we can avoid disappointment or failure. But life refuses to be mastered.

What often happens when we grip too tightly?

- Relationships suffocate.

- Creativity stalls.

- Our bodies rebel.

- We grow anxious, brittle, and exhausted.

Letting go is not abandoning responsibility. It's recognizing where responsibility ends.

It's saying: *I will show up, do the work, and speak the truth—but I will not pretend that I control the outcome.*

What Surrender Actually Looks Like

- **In relationships:** Letting someone be who they are without trying to edit them. Loving without rescuing. Setting boundaries without revenge.

- **In work:** Doing your best and releasing the need for praise or perfect outcomes. Admitting what you don't know. Trusting others to carry their part.

- **In parenting:** Teaching through example and presence, not through domination. Allowing children to fail—and learn.

- **In the self:** Listening instead of fixing. Resting without guilt. Trusting your intuition even when there's no spreadsheet to back it up.

Surrender isn't the absence of effort. It's the absence of *force*.

Why It's So Hard

Letting go feels dangerous because we've linked control to safety, identity, and even morality. We ask: *If I'm not in control, who am I? What if everything falls apart?*

But here's the deeper question: *What if everything has already fallen apart because of control?*

So much of our stress comes not from life itself, but from resisting how life actually is.

Surrender begins when we stop fighting the truth.

The Gifts of Letting Go

Once we release the compulsion to control, several things begin to emerge—quietly, almost miraculously:

- **Clarity**: Without the noise of fear and fixation, we can actually hear ourselves think and feel.

- **Connection**: People draw closer when they feel trusted, not managed.

- **Creativity**: New ideas flow when we stop obsessing over doing things "right."

- **Resilience**: We bounce back faster because we're not crushed by unmet expectations.

But perhaps the greatest gift is *inner peace*. The steady confidence that, come what may, we will meet life with openness, integrity, and presence.

Surrender as Strength

The most powerful people you've met likely had this quality: they didn't need to control the room to influence it. They didn't need everyone's approval to act with clarity. They didn't chase outcomes—they aligned with values.

This is the paradox: when we stop trying to control everything, we become more powerful. Not because we dominate, but because we become deeply aligned with what matters most.

Surrender is not weak. It is the foundation of true power.

In the final chapter, we will explore what it means to reclaim peace—not by conquering, but by living from a deeper, wiser center.

Chapter 9: Control in the Digital Age

We live in an age where control has taken on a new shape—one coded in algorithms, disguised as convenience, and delivered in push notifications.

Not long ago, control meant owning land, commanding armies, or holding office. Today, it often means owning data. And unlike traditional power, this form of control is quieter, subtler—yet far more pervasive. It doesn't knock on your door or announce itself. It just *loads*… quickly, seamlessly, in the background.

The Comfort of Convenience, the Cost of Consent

We didn't hand over our autonomy all at once. It happened gradually. With every "I Agree" we clicked without reading, with every location permission we allowed, and with every moment we told ourselves, *It's just an app.*

What we got in return was convenience. Directions to anywhere. Groceries in minutes. Friends from school, college, and countries we've never been to—just a click away.

But here's the catch: convenience makes control feel like a choice.

In reality, our digital lives are constantly being shaped by forces we don't fully see. The apps we use are not just tools; they're feedback loops, designed to learn from us, predict us, and, eventually, influence us.

Surveillance You Can't See

George Orwell imagined a world where Big Brother would watch us through cameras on every wall. What he didn't foresee was that we'd *buy* the cameras ourselves, call them "smart," and install them in our homes.

Surveillance today doesn't need force. It runs on incentives. Free apps. Smart assistants. Personalized ads. Every tap, scroll, like, and pause is a data point. And these data points build a version of you that corporations and governments can know, model, and—yes—manipulate.

You are being watched. But more than that, you are being *understood*. Intimately. Precisely. Predictively.

And the most dangerous part? It doesn't feel dangerous at all.

Algorithms Don't Sleep

An algorithm has no ideology. No agenda. No feelings. It just optimizes. For clicks. For engagement. For time spent on screen. But what it *ends up* optimizing is behavior.

You click on one fitness video, and suddenly your feed is health and hustle. You engage with one controversial post, and the next day you're swimming in polarizing content. You buy a book about parenting, and now every ad treats you like you have three toddlers at home.

It's not evil. It's just math. But this math shapes what you believe, who you trust, and even how you see the world.

What kind of control is this—where your choices are your own, but also not quite?

Social Media: A Stage and a Cage

Social media sold us the dream of having a voice. And at first, it felt like a revolution. You could speak, be heard, matter.

But slowly, that voice got tied to metrics—likes, shares, views. And once that happened, self-expression turned into performance. We began optimizing *ourselves*—our words, our photos, our opinions—for the algorithm.

We don't just share anymore. We *curate*.

And here's the irony: in a place where everyone has a voice, only a few get heard. The algorithm decides. It amplifies what keeps people scrolling—not necessarily what's true, thoughtful, or kind.

You feel in control, but the script is being written elsewhere.

The Illusion of Choice

Think about your Netflix recommendations. Your YouTube feed. Your Google search results. They all *feel* like neutral platforms, giving you endless options. But those options are filtered, ranked, and served based on past behavior.

And so, your "choices" become echoes. Reinforcements of what you already clicked, liked, or watched. You think you're exploring. But you're mostly orbiting.

This is the heart of the illusion: the more options we have, the freer we feel—while the system silently narrows what we see.

The Age of AI: Predict, Persuade, Decide

With the rise of artificial intelligence, this illusion becomes even more intricate. AI doesn't just analyze what we've done; it anticipates what we *will* do.

It can write like us. Talk like us. Sell to us. Even argue with us.

And yet, it remains invisible. We rarely know which decisions were made by humans, and which were nudged by code. Did you choose that product because you wanted it, or because a model knew you would? Did you read that article, or was it simply pushed into your path before you could look away?

We talk about machine learning. But maybe we should ask what *we're* learning—or unlearning—in return.

When Control Feels Like Safety

The strange thing is, many of us *want* this. We want the algorithm to know our taste in music. We want maps to tell us the fastest route. We want Netflix to guess our mood.

And we want our feeds to show us things we already agree with—because it's easier that way.

The digital world offers us the kind of control that feels gentle, intuitive, responsive. But in making everything so easy, it also makes us less aware of how little we're actually choosing.

Control has become comfortable. Predictable. Painless.

And that's exactly why it's so powerful.

The Mirror We Didn't Expect

In the end, technology didn't create our desire for control—it simply gave it new clothes. New speed. New reach. And perhaps, a new cost.

We thought we were building tools. But the tools began to shape us. We sought efficiency and ended up trading attention. We craved connection and ended up feeling watched. We chased control—and slowly handed it over.

We are not helpless. We can log out. We can read the fine print. We can pause and reflect. But first, we must a what it is.Because the most dangerous control is not the one taken from us—but the one we never realized we gave away.

Chapter 10: The Psychology of Surrender

Why Letting Go Can Be More Powerful Than Holding On

We're taught to hold on. To stay strong. To power through. That the tight grip of control is the only thing standing between us and chaos.

But what if the opposite were true?

What if, in trying to control everything—our emotions, our careers, our relationships, even our thoughts—we're creating the very suffering we're trying to avoid?

This is the paradox: Sometimes, the greatest strength lies not in holding on, but in letting go.

The Trap of Mental Control

In psychology, there's a term called *experiential avoidance*—our tendency to try to suppress or escape uncomfortable thoughts, feelings, or sensations. We try to "manage" our anxiety. We push away sadness. We distract ourselves from guilt or fear.

And for a while, it works. But the more we resist, the more these experiences persist. What we fight tends to fight back.

You try not to think about something—and it comes back louder. You try to force happiness—and end up more frustrated. You try to control your mind—and it rebels.

Control becomes a mental tug-of-war. And the harder you pull, the more exhausted you become.

Buddhism: The Wisdom of Non-Attachment

Long before psychology gave it terms and frameworks, Buddhism offered an insight that feels radical even today: *The root of suffering is attachment*—to outcomes, to identities, to desires.

But attachment is really just another form of control. We cling to what we want, push away what we fear, and build entire identities around what we think life should look like.

Suffering, the Buddha taught, isn't just about pain. It's about our refusal to let life flow. Our need to steer, shape, and structure every experience to fit a narrative that makes us feel secure.

Freedom, then, is not found in mastering the world—but in loosening our grip on it.

Acceptance and Commitment Therapy: A Modern Approach to Ancient Wisdom

In recent decades, modern therapy has begun echoing these ancient truths. Acceptance and Commitment Therapy (ACT) teaches us not to control our thoughts, but to *notice* them. Not to suppress our emotions, but to *make space* for them.

ACT asks a deceptively simple question: "Is this struggle helping you live a life that matters?"

Often, our pursuit of control isn't about values—it's about fear. Fear of discomfort. Fear of uncertainty.

Fear of failure. But when we let go of the need to control those fears, they lose their grip on us.

It's not about giving up. It's about *showing up*—fully, honestly, even when things are hard.

You stop wrestling with the storm and start learning how to walk in the rain.

Surrender Is Not Defeat

Let's be clear: surrender is not passivity. It's not apathy or helplessness or "giving up." That's resignation.

Surrender is presence. It's saying, "This is what is, right now. I don't have to like it. But I don't have to fight it either."

It's the difference between swimming upstream and floating with the current—not because you're lazy, but because you've realized the river doesn't care how tired you are.

Paradoxically, surrender often brings clarity. Once we stop trying to force life into a shape, we can finally see it for what it is—and act from a place of grounded wisdom, not panic.

Letting Go of the Inner Judge

So much of our internal control comes from one voice: the inner judge.

It tells us we're not doing enough. That we should be better, faster, calmer, thinner, smarter. That we're behind. That others are ahead. That we need to fix ourselves before we can be happy.

But this judge is not our truth. It's a patchwork of fear, culture, comparison, and past pain. And trying to control ourselves to meet its impossible standards is a battle we will always lose.

Letting go means letting that voice speak—but not letting it rule. It means turning down its volume, and tuning in to something softer: values, compassion, curiosity.

That's not weakness. That's healing.

When Surrender Becomes Power

Think of the most profound moments in life—grief, love, birth, death, awe. They are bigger than us. They humble us. And in those moments, control feels irrelevant.

You don't *manage* falling in love. You don't *optimize* grief. You don't *engineer* awe.

You surrender to it. And in doing so, you expand.

True freedom doesn't come from controlling the chaos. It comes from learning to be *with it*, without losing ourselves.

That's the kind of control worth chasing—not over the world, but within ourselves.

Closing Reflection:

We spend so much of our lives tightening our fists—on relationships, on outcomes, on identities. But sometimes, peace doesn't come when we gain more control. It comes when we stop needing it so badly.

The mind, it turns out, is not a machine to master. It's a wild horse to ride. And perhaps the wisest thing we can do is loosen the reins, trust our direction, and let the journey unfold.

Because letting go isn't the end of control. It's the beginning of something far more powerful: freedom.

Chapter 11: The Price of Power in Relationships

Why Control Often Comes at the Cost of Connection
Power is seductive. In politics, in business—and yes, in love.

It sneaks into our relationships not always with grand displays, but through subtle expectations, quiet rules, and unspoken ultimatums. We don't always mean to control others. But somewhere between caring deeply and fearing loss, control begins to masquerade as love.

We want to be heard. To be understood. To be respected. But too often, we also want to be *right*. And when being right becomes more important than being close, connection quietly slips away.

When Love Becomes a Battlefield

We often think of control in relationships as something dramatic—manipulation, dominance, jealousy. But control wears many masks.

Sometimes, it looks like trying to change our partner "for their own good."
Sometimes, it sounds like giving the silent treatment until we get our way.
Sometimes, it hides behind phrases like "I just know what's best" or "Why can't you see I'm doing this for us?"

At its core, control comes from fear: fear of being abandoned, betrayed, misunderstood, or irrelevant. So we build walls. Or we micromanage. Or we set impossible standards—because if everything goes *our* way, maybe we won't get hurt.

But control doesn't protect intimacy. It poisons it.

Power vs. Partnership

There's a difference between influence and control. Between mutual respect and quiet coercion. Between a relationship built on trust and one built on strategy.

Power dynamics show up in all kinds of partnerships—not just romantic ones. Parents try to control children. Friends try to fix each other. Leaders try to mold their teams. The moment one person starts managing the other like a problem to solve, the balance shifts.

Relationships are meant to be fluid. Alive. They're not projects. They're not puzzles. They're two people meeting each other as they are—imperfect, evolving, and *free*.

When one person always has to win, both eventually lose.

Control Feels Safe. Vulnerability *Is* Safe.

Control is often a substitute for vulnerability.

It's easier to tell someone how they should behave than to say, "When you did that, I felt scared."

It's easier to demand change than to admit, "I feel insecure."

It's easier to shut down than to say, "I need your reassurance."

But vulnerability—real, unpolished honesty—is where intimacy grows. It's the place where control becomes unnecessary, because connection takes over.

Love isn't about managing someone's behavior. It's about understanding their heart.

The Illusion of the Upper Hand

In any relationship, the moment we start keeping score, we've already lost the plot.

Who gave more. Who tried harder. Who apologized last. Who had the final say.

It's a trap—and it gives the illusion that having the upper hand is somehow winning. But love is not a power game. It's not about leverage. It's about presence.

When we treat relationships like negotiations, we lose the warmth. When we treat them like territory to defend, we lose the tenderness. And when we treat love like a performance to be judged, we forget how to simply *be* with each other.

The need to control often comes from a place of past pain. But healing doesn't come from control. It comes from safety. And safety is built through trust, not tactics.

Letting People Be Themselves

One of the most radical acts of love is letting someone be who they are—even when it's inconvenient, uncomfortable, or not what we expected.

Not because we approve of every decision. But because we respect their right to decide.

This doesn't mean accepting harm or staying silent about what matters. It means drawing boundaries without building cages. It means standing up for ourselves without standing *over* someone else.

It means loving without possession.

Because control might get us compliance—but it won't get us closeness.

What Real Power Looks Like

Real power in relationships isn't about dominating. It's about listening when it's hard. Apologizing when you're right. Holding space when you're scared. Letting go when holding on would only hurt both of you.

It's the power to choose love over ego. Curiosity over assumptions. Peace over pride.

It's not loud or flashy. It doesn't always win arguments. But it wins trust. And that, in the long run, is everything.

Closing Reflection: We chase control in relationships to feel safe. But true safety doesn't come from managing others—it comes from being able to show up as ourselves, and letting others do the same. Love isn't about perfect behavior. It's about presence. Kindness. Flexibility. And above all, freedom. Because at the end of the day, the only relationship worth holding on to—is one where no one has to be held down.

Chapter 12: When Control Becomes Chaos

We like to think that control brings stability. That if we plan enough, manage enough, anticipate enough—we can outsmart uncertainty.

But here's the strange truth: the tighter we hold the reins, the more life seems to buck.

Our obsession with control doesn't eliminate chaos. It often *creates* it.

Not suddenly. Not dramatically. But slowly, like a knot pulled tighter and tighter—until something snaps.

The Domino Effect of Micromanagement

Imagine trying to control every element of your day: every word in a meeting, every calorie you eat, every email response, every unpredictable thing people might say or do.

At first, it feels powerful. You're on top of things. Organized. In charge.

But soon, decisions pile up. Flexibility disappears. The smallest disruptions feel catastrophic. You start reacting to the *threat* of disorder, not the reality of it.

This is how micromanagement—whether of tasks, people, or emotions—spirals into burnout.

The more you try to manage, the more there *is* to manage. Until the system you're trying to control becomes the very chaos you're trying to avoid.

Control as a Coping Mechanism

Control is often our armor. It gives us the illusion of protection in a world that's too big, too fast, too unpredictable.

People who've experienced trauma, instability, or emotional neglect often develop hyper-control as a survival strategy. And in the short term, it works. It gives them clarity. Predictability. A feeling of safety.

But the long-term cost is high.

Relationships suffer. Creativity dries up. Spontaneity becomes terrifying. We begin to confuse anxiety with responsibility. And slowly, we lose touch with the parts of life that *can't* be controlled—but are worth experiencing anyway.

Love. Trust. Surprise. Growth.

Control gives us safety. But it can also take away life

The Myth of the Master Plan

Modern life feeds our control addiction. Productivity apps. Life hacks. Calendar blocks. Self-help mantras. Vision boards.

None of these are bad on their own. But when they become tools for controlling every variable—every outcome—we start living in a future that doesn't exist.

We don't just plan for contingencies. We try to outwit *life itself*. As if the right combination of effort and foresight will finally secure our peace.

But life doesn't work that way.

Plans fall through. Markets crash. People change. Storms arrive without warning. And if our peace depends on the plan going perfectly, then peace will always be just out of reach.

We weren't designed to *conquer* life. We were designed to *engage* with it—imperfectly, vulnerably, fully.

When Control Backfires

Here's what control doesn't tell you: it's fragile.

It depends on everything staying within your parameters. But real life rarely does.

The parent who controls every aspect of a child's life eventually faces rebellion—or quiet resentment.
The partner who monitors every word and movement of their loved one ends up alone.
The professional who never delegates, never rests, and never trusts others often burns out—or breaks down.

In each case, control was meant to prevent pain. But it often *causes* it.

Not because control is evil. But because it has limits. And when we ignore those limits, the consequences are inevitable.

From Rigidity to Resilience

So what's the alternative? Chaos?

Not at all. The answer isn't to abandon structure—it's to replace *rigidity* with *resilience*.

Resilience doesn't mean letting life trample over you. It means learning how to bend without breaking. To adapt without collapsing. To experience uncertainty without losing your center.

Instead of controlling the storm, you learn to sail through it.

Instead of scripting every outcome, you prepare yourself to *respond*—not just *react*—to whatever arises.

This shift is quiet but radical. It's the difference between living in fear of what might go wrong… and living in trust that you can handle what does.

The Wisdom of Unraveling

Sometimes the chaos we fear is exactly what we need.

The relationship that falls apart teaches us what real connection means.
The job we lose opens the door to our real calling.
The identity we clung to crumbles—and we discover who we really are beneath it.

Control resists these unraveling. But wisdom welcomes them.

Because chaos, while uncomfortable, is also honest. It reveals what was never truly in our control to begin with. And in that revelation, something sacred happens:

We stop trying to manage the waves—and start learning how to surf.

Closing Reflection: Control promises safety. But often delivers stress. It promises certainty. But often fuels anxiety. It promises order. But can end in chaos. What if the real path to peace isn't more control—but more courage? The courage to face the unknown. To risk imperfection. To loosen the grip. To allow life to be messy, unpredictable—and still beautiful. Because in the end, it's not control that brings calm. It's *trust*—in yourself, in life, in your ability to meet the moment with grace.

Conclusion: Reclaiming Peace Without Control

We began this journey with a paradox: that the more we try to control life, the more out of control we often feel. That in our pursuit of power—over others, over ourselves, over uncertainty—we may be forfeiting the very things we long for most: connection, clarity, and peace.

What we've uncovered in these chapters is not just a critique of control, but an invitation to a new way of living. A life not dominated by fear and perfectionism, but guided by purpose, presence, and trust.

Because here is the truth:

- Control is exhausting.

- Influence is empowering.

- Surrender is liberating.

The illusion of control thrives in a culture that worships productivity, certainty, and self-sufficiency. But beneath the surface, many of us are tired. Tired of pretending to have it all together. Tired of chasing outcomes that leave us empty. Tired of managing impressions, micromanaging life, and missing the actual moments that matter.

Reclaiming peace means something radical in today's world: it means **not always needing to fix, win, or know.** It means choosing to *feel* instead of numb, to *listen* instead of dictate, to *be* instead of constantly *do*.

This isn't passivity. It's power of a different kind—a quiet, unshakeable kind.

You Are Not Your Control

The ego convinces us that control equals identity. That without the constant managing of roles, responsibilities, and results, we'll somehow dissolve into irrelevance.

But you are not your job title. You are not your to-do list. You are not your perfect parenting, your clean inbox, or your controlled emotions.

You are something far more spacious: a human being, in process. Fallible, beautiful, evolving.

You don't have to earn your worth through control. You don't have to orchestrate your life into a performance. You don't have to be "on top of it all" to be okay.

What Peace Really Is

Peace is not the absence of problems. It is the absence of *panic in the face of problems*.

It's the ability to say, "This is hard—and I can handle it."
"This didn't go as planned—and I'm still here."
"I don't have control—but I do have a choice."

Peace comes when we trade the illusion of certainty for the practice of presence. When we drop the armor and discover that vulnerability is not the opposite of power—it is the source of it.

Living the Shift

If you take one thing from this book, let it be this:

Control is a story. Presence is a practice.

The story of control will always be seductive. But presence—real, grounded, messy presence—is what makes life worth living. It's what builds trust. It's what fosters change. It's what allows you to breathe again.

Letting go is not a one-time act. It's a rhythm. A way of relating to life, people, and yourself with more compassion than critique, more curiosity than command.

Some days, you'll fall back into the grip. That's okay. Just notice it. Smile. Release.

Come back to the truth: you are not here to dominate life.

You are here to meet it fully, love deeply, and let go— again and again. That is where peace lives

www.ingramcontent.com/pod-product-compliance
Lightning Source LLC
Chambersburg PA
CBHW031502150726
47990CB00007B/2842